Mayan Pyramid At
Cichén-Itzá

FACES AND PLACES

MEXICO

Crossroads Elementary Library

BY MARY BERENDES

THE CHILD'S WORLD®

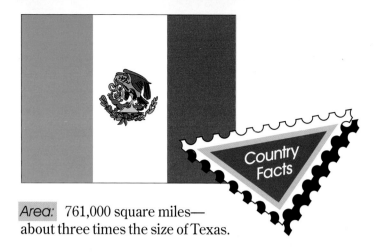

Country Facts

Area: 761,000 square miles—
about three times the size of Texas.

Population: About 95 million people.

Capital City: Mexico City.

Other Important Cities: Guadalajara, Monterrey, Puebla, León,
Ciudad Juárez, Tijuana.

Money: The peso.

National Language: Spanish. There are also many Indian languages.

National Song: "Himno Nacional de Mexico" or "National Anthem of Mexico".

National Holiday: Independence Day on September 16.

National Flag: Three stripes of red, white, and green. The white stripe has the
national coat of arms in the middle. The green stripe stands for hope. The white
stripe stands for Mexico's purity. The red stripe stands for those who died
fighting for Mexico's independence.

Head of Government: President Ernesto Zedillo Ponce de León.

Text copyright © 1998 by The Child's World®, Inc.
All rights reserved. No part of this book may be reproduced
or utilized in any form or by any means without written
permission from the publisher.
Printed in the United States of America.

Library of Congress Cataloging-in-Publication Data
Berendes, Mary.
Mexico / by Mary Berendes.
Series: "Faces and Places".
p. cm.
Includes index.
Summary: Describes the geography, history,
people, and customs of Mexico
ISBN 1-56766-372-9 (hard cover, library bound)

1. Mexico — Description and travel — Juvenile literature.
2. Mexico — Social life and customs — Juvenile literature.
[1. Mexico.] I. Title.

F1216.5.B47 1998
972 — dc20

96-30665
CIP
AC

GRAPHIC DESIGN
Robert A. Honey, Seattle

PHOTO RESEARCH
James R. Rothaus / James R. Rothaus & Associates

ELECTRONIC PRE–PRESS PRODUCTION
Robert E. Bonaker / Graphic Design & Consulting Co.

PHOTOGRAPHY
Cover photo: Boy Carries Flowers by Danny Lehman/©Corbis

Table
of
Contents

CHAPTER	PAGE

Imagine that you could fly high above Earth. What do you think you would see? If you looked down, you would see some huge land areas surrounded by water. These land areas are called continents. Some continents are made up of many different countries.

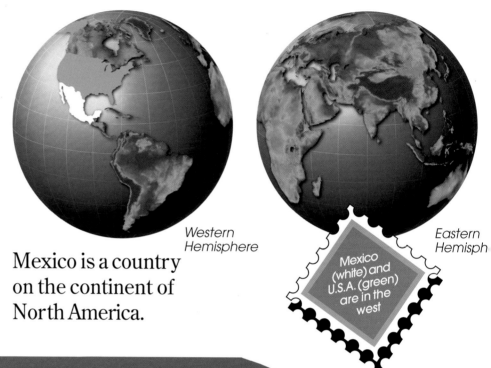

Western Hemisphere

Eastern Hemisph

Mexico is a country on the continent of North America.

Mexico (white) and U.S.A. (green) are in the west

Arctic Ocean

NORTH AMERICA

United States of America

Mexico

Pacific Ocean

Atlantic Ocean

SOUTH AMERICA

EUROPE

ASIA

AFRICA

Indian Ocean

Pacific Ocean

AUSTRALIA

ANTARCTICA

The World Shown Flat

Close-Up
of
Mexico

UNITED STATES OF
AMERICA

Gulf
Of
Mexico

MEXICO

BELIZE

GUATEMALA

Pacific
Ocean

BAJA

Sierra Madre Occidental

Sierra Madre Oriental

Desert Plateau

Gulf Of Mexico

♣ Chichén-Itzá

Coba ♣

Tom Bean/Corbis

Boojum Trees And Cacti On Desert Plateau

There are many different kinds of land in Mexico. There are mountains and jungles. There are plains and deserts. There are even beaches! Much of Mexico is a huge, flat area called a plateau. A plateau is an area of land that is higher than the areas of land around it. Mexico's plateau is bordered by two chains of mountains—one in the west and one in the east. They are called the Sierra Madres.

Charles & Josette Lenars/Corbis

Playa el Amor In Baja

The Purcell Team/Corbis

Cypress Trees On Gulf Of Mexico

Richard A. Cooke III/Corbis

Jungle Around Cone Pyramid At Coba

Jaguar At Rest Near Comitán

Cordaiy Photo Library Ltd./Corbis

David Muench/Corbis

Many types of plants live in Mexico. In the dry north, cactus and mesquite plants grow. In other areas of Mexico, thick jungles cover the land. High in the mountains, oak and pine trees grow.

Just like the plants, the animals that live in Mexico are different in each part of the country. Wolves and coyotes are found in the north. In the mountain forests, jaguars, bears, and pumas roam. Snakes, parrots, monkeys, and lizards live in Mexico's jungles. Many types of insects and fish can be found in Mexico, too.

Cacti And City Of Rocks

Palm Trees And Birds At Coyuca de Benitez

Danny Lehman/©Corbis

Coyotes
Cactus
Dry North

Puerto
Vallarta

Coyuca
de Benitez

Jungles

Comitán

Iguana
And Sunbather
Near Puerto
Vallarta

Mayan Temple Of Seven Dolls

Toltecs
Aztecs
Olmecs •Villahermosa
Uxmal
Mayas
•Cozumel

Jonathan Blair/Corbis

Aztec Temple Near Cozumel

Kevin Morris/Corbis

Long Ago

The First People came to Mexico thousands of years ago. They had names such as the Olmecs, Toltecs, Maya and Aztecs. These groups built huge cities out of stone. They built pyramids and palaces and temples. The First People were so good at building, some of the things they built are still standing today!

In the 1500s, explorers from other countries began arriving in Mexico. They were looking for riches and for new places to live. Some explorers from Spain told their king about the beautiful country of Mexico. He wanted it to be a part of his kingdom. The country of Spain took away the land from the First People. Spain ruled Mexico for 300 years.

Mayan Ruins At Uxmal

Nik Wheeler/Corbis

Colossal Olmec Head At Villahermosa

Charles & Josette Lenars/Corbis

Mexico Today

Today, Mexicans have their own government. They have a president instead of a king. The president and the government make laws that keep Mexico safe.

Planting Corn In Munereachic

Phil Schermeister/Corbis

Boy Carrying Hoes Near Copper Canyon

The Mexican people try to get along with one another. But not all people are treated fairly in Mexico. Many of the relatives of the First People, called Indians, are forced to live in poor areas. They cannot get very good jobs.

To help, the government has given Indians some of the land their relatives once owned. But these areas are still very poor. Many of the people who live there must work in coffee or vegetable fields to make enough money to live.

Phil Schermeister/Corbis

Chiapa Indian Family

Macduff Everton/Corbis

Chiapas
Munereachic
Copper
Canyon

YUCATAN

Mayas

Mayan
Women And
Child From
Yucatan

Danny Lehman/© Corbis

Beach
Hotels
In
Acapulco

Ciudad Juárez

Puerto
Vallarta

Acapulco

Mitla

Danny Lehman/© Corbis

The Mexican population is made up of three groups. The Spanish people are relatives of the first Spanish settlers. The Indians are another group. The people in Mexico who have both Indian and Spanish relatives are called mestizos. Most Mexicans are mestizos.

Almost all of Mexico's people live on the plateau or in the mountains. Areas that are close to the United States or along beaches are growing, too. In these areas, Mexicans can find lots of jobs to do. They can also find places to build new homes.

Spanish Style Church And Cacti At Mitla

Nik Wheeler/Corbis

Cuidad Juárez On The United States Border

Richard Bickel/Corbis

Hillside Living In Puerto Villarta

Morton Beebe-S.F./Corbis

ADMIT ONE

**City Life
And
Country
Life**

ADMIT ONE

Indian
Mud Brick
House In
Munereachic

Phil Schermeister/Corbis

Most Mexicans live in the city. In the city, people can find jobs to do and places to buy things. Hundreds of people move into Mexico's cities every day. Sometimes, Mexico's cities are so crowded, there are not enough places for the newcomers to live.

Many country people live in villages. They build houses with sticks and mud. Some people make their houses out of adobe (UH–DOH–bee). Adobe is a type of brick that is made from mixing straw with mud. Many country people work on farms. Others travel to the cities to work.

Colorful Houses Of
Zihuatanejo

The Purcell Team/Corbis

Poor
Housing In
Mexico
City

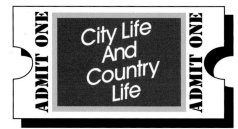

Sergio Dorantes/© Corbis

Morton Beebe-S.F./Corbis

Munereachic

Mexico City

Zihuatanejo

Only The Very Rich
Can Afford
This House

Government
School
Classroom
Near
Monterrey

Monterrey•

University
of Mexico• •Veracruz

Some Classes Are Taught Outdoors

When Mexican children are four years old, they begin school. They attend two years of preschool and kindergarten. There they learn things such as games, singing, and dancing. These are activities that will help them as they get older. When children turn six years old, they begin elementary school. They learn math, science, and social studies just as you do. Most students in Mexico go to school until they are 15 years old.

Dan Guravich/Corbis

Mexico's official language is Spanish. It was brought over by the Spanish explorers. There are also many Indian languages. They are spoken in the Indian villages. Both kinds of languages are very old. They are also very beautiful.

Students Wear Uniforms To This School In Veracruz

Stephanie Maze/Corbis

Owen Franken/Corbis

Orozco Mural On The University Of Mexico Library

Crossroads Elementary Library

In Mexico, there are many jobs to do. Some people work on farms that produce coffee, fruit, or vegetables. Others make blankets and pottery to sell. Many people work in shops, hotels, and restaurants. And Mexico's cities have factories that make everything from paper to clothes. Mexico is a busy place!

Waitress In Mexico City

Danny Lehman/© Corbis

Harvesting Onions Near Popocatepetl Volcano

Sergio Dorantes/© Corbis

Yucatan Men Drying Sisal Fibers For Making Rope

Macduff Everton/Corbis

Danny Lehman/© Corbis

Mexico City

YUCATAN

+ *Popocatepetl*

Acapulco

Fishermen
Pull In
A Net At
Acapulco

Dining Room In
Oaxaca
Home

Guadalajara • • Mexico City

Oaxaca •

Food

Many dishes in Mexico are made with tortillas (tor–TEE–yus) Tortillas are like flat pancakes that are made out of corn. They are used in dishes such as tacos and enchiladas. Many Mexican dishes are made with beans, corn, tomatoes, and peppers.

Food Stand In Mexico City Market

Danny Lehman/© Corbis

Making A Tortilla In Guadalajara

Dave G. Houser/Corbis

In Mexico, eating slowly and enjoying your food is very important. The meal is a time to relax and talk with friends and family. The biggest meal of the day is lunch. It is served around 2:00 in the afternoon. A light supper is served just before bedtime.

Danny Lehman/© Corbis

Pancake Stand In Mexico City

Pastimes

ADMIT ONE · ADMIT ONE

Mexicans love sports, especially soccer. They also like to watch baseball, boxing, and a fast game called jai alai (HIGH LIE). Jai alai is similar to racquetball that is played in the United States.

Bullfight In Tijuana

Nik Wheeler/Corbis

One of the oldest sports in Mexico is bullfighting. In this pastime, a man called a matador (MA–tuh–dor) stands in a ring with an angry bull. He waves a bright cape at the bull, hoping the bull will charge. When it does, the matador quickly moves out of the way. Bullfighting takes bravery and skill. If the matador moves the wrong way, the bull can hurt him. Some people think bullfighting is mean. That's because at the end of a bullfight, the bull usually dies.

Soccer Game In Guerrero

Children Playing In Stream Near San Blas

Nik Wheeler/Corbis

Dave G. Houser/Corbis

World Cup
Soccer
Opening
Ceremonies
In
Mexico City

Day Of The Dead
Costume In
Chihuahua

Chihuahua

Cancun

Mexico City •

Mayans

• Xochicalco

Sergio Dorantes/© Corbis

Holidays

ADMIT ONE · ADMIT ONE

Mexicans celebrate many of the same holidays as we do. One special holiday is The Day of the Dead. It is celebrated from October 31 to November 2. During this special time, people remember loved ones who have died. They bake special bread, eat candy skeletons, and have picnics in cemeteries. In Mexico, The Day of the Dead is a time to remember the dead with joy instead of sadness.

Mexico is a beautiful country that is filled with bright colors and friendly people. Perhaps one day you will climb to the top of a pyramid built by the First People. Or maybe you will want to visit one of Mexico's sunny beaches. Wherever you go, and whatever you do, Mexico is sure to make you smile.

Costumed Pilgrim In Mexico City

Danny Lehman/© Corbis

Surfers At Cancun

Kelly-Mooney/Corbis

Charles & Josette Lenars/Corbis

Ruins Of Mayan Temple

Did You Know?

Mexico is really called "The United Mexican States." People just say "Mexico" for short.

Vanilla and chocolate originally came from Mexico.

Mexicans hang piñatas (pin–YAH–tuhs) from long strings for special days. A piñata is a brightly colored bag filled with toys and candy. Blindfolded children try to hit the piñata with a stick to break it open. When the piñata breaks, toys and candy spill out for everyone to enjoy!

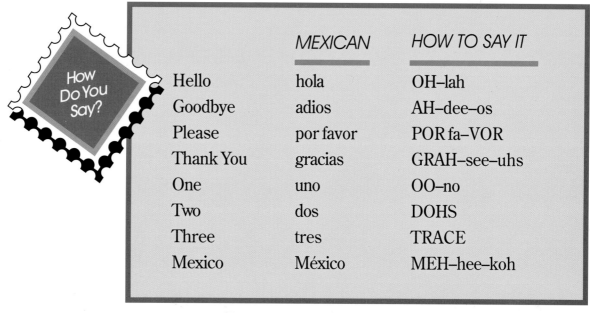

How Do You Say?

	MEXICAN	HOW TO SAY IT
Hello	hola	OH–lah
Goodbye	adios	AH–dee–os
Please	por favor	POR fa–VOR
Thank You	gracias	GRAH–see–uhs
One	uno	OO–no
Two	dos	DOHS
Three	tres	TRACE
Mexico	México	MEH–hee–koh

adobe (uh–DOH–bee)
Adobe is a brick that is made from mud and straw.
In Mexico, some people build houses out of adobe.

continent (KON–tuh–nent)
Most of the land areas on Earth are divided up into huge sections
called continents. Mexico is on the continent of North America.

mestizos (meh–STEE–zohs)
Mestizos are Mexicans who have both Indian and Spanish relatives.
Most Mexicans are mestizos.

plateau (pla–TOH)
A plateau is an area that is higher than the areas of land around it.
Mexico's plateau is bordered by the Sierra Madre mountains.

tortilla (tor–TEE–yuh)
A tortilla is a round, flat pancake that is made of corn. Tortillas are
used in many Mexican dishes.

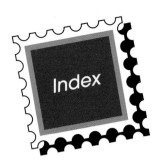